WORDS FROM THE HOLY BIBLE

CHOICES

OUT

THE

GOOD

BOOK

FROM A LEARNERS JOURNAL

WORDS FROM THE HOLY BIBLE
CHOICES OUT THE GOOD BOOK FROM A LEARNER'S JOURNAL.

iUniverse books may be ordered through booksellers or by contacting:

iUniverse
1663 Liberty Drive
Bloomington, IN 47403
www.iuniverse.com
844-349-9409

ISBN: 978-1-5320-6322-0 (sc)
ISBN: 978-1-5320-6323-7 (e)

Print information available on the last page.

iUniverse rev. date: 10/30/2020

Table Of Contents

INTRODUCTION

By

Damitri Lashawn Franklin

The Holy Bible, The Greatest Book Of All Time, The Holy Bible is truth

and many people have read it and put their trust in it just as they've put

their trust and faith in God. Jesus Christ Our Lord And Savior Of The World

died for our sins whom I believe in. I read the Holy Bible 7 times in 32 months,

and the fastest I've read it was 61 days. I've chosen many scripture out

of the Old Testament and New Testament, I've also chosen many chapters out

of the Old Testament and New Testament. I've kept them to help me through

life and you too. This is to get every individual to Heaven when they die and not Hell,

cause life and individual souls is not a game. Some of the words from the

Holy Bible you will not understand so buy a dictionary to help guide you and

comprehend the scripture. I've learned so so much from the Holy Bible and I

wouldn't of been capable of putting this together if it wasn't for it, and

God The Creator. Jesus Christ Our Lord And Savior To All, Let His Spirit

Guide Us And Walk With Us All On Gods Earth.

May The Blessings Of God Be On Us All, Peace And Goodwill Toward All Mankind.

Analyzed and Peaced by *Damitri Franklin* Bless You

1

The Paragraph Page Here Explains The Content Of A Scripture

This section here I give you the colors of the scripture I have marked out

in my bible. Some scripture are highlighted yellow, orange, green, blue, pink,

and the purple you see it's better to mark it as yellow cause the purple wasn't

good highlight ink for my bible. Also you'll see next to some scripture

stars up top, checkmarks, exclamation marks, and question marks.

GW stands for Gods Words and JW stands for Jesus Words. Now for

explaining the different colors, if you see no stars next to the scripture

that means that scripture is yellow, if you see one star next to the scripture

that means it's yellow also, if you see two stars next to the scripture

that means that scripture is orange. Green scripture to me means strength

or attention. Blue scripture to me means the sky or out of this world.

Pink scripture to me means forgiveness, love, or humbleness.

Yellow scripture to me means important or more important.

Orange scripture to me means more important. Checkmarks important,

Stars Up Top important, but all in all, all is important.

May The Blessings Of God Be On Us All, Peace And Goodwill Toward All Mankind.

Now Let's All Meditate On Righteous Living And Gods Love

Chapters I've Picked Out Some Books Of The Old Testament

Genesis (Chapters 1,3,4,5,6)

Leviticus (Chapters 12,26,23-GW to Moses about 1ˢᵗ & 7ᵗʰ month. Holy Convocations)

Deuteronomy (Chapters 6,24,28 Don't Forsake God,30,31,32)

Joshua (Chapter 23★)

I Samuel (Chapter 17 David vs. Goliath)

II Samuel (Chapter 7)

II Kings (Chapter 9)

I Chronicles (Chapter 17)

II Chronicles (Chapters 6,32)

Psalms (Chapters 2,3,18,24,25,47,76,82,96,109,136)

Proverbs "The Book of Wisdom" (Read All Chapters) (Chapters 3,4,13,17,23,25,27)

Ecclesiastes (Chapters 3,7,8,9)

Song of Solomon (Chapter 2)

Isaiah (Chapters 13,14,20,25,37,40,41,42,52,54★✳★,63)

Jeremiah (Chapters 45,48 O Moab!,51 Babylon)

Ezekiel (Chapters 16,18,19 A Lamentation,33,45)

Daniel (Chapters 11,12)

Micah (Chapter 7)

Nahum (Chapter 1)

Zechariah (Read All Chapters) (Chapter 7)

Chapters I've Picked Out Some Books Of The New Testament

St. Matthew (Chapters 5jw,10,15,19,23)

St. Luke (Chapters 4,12,13,14,15,16,17,18)

St. John (Chapters 1 The Son of God!,2,6 jw,13,15,16,17 jw night prayer)

Acts (Chapters 3,4,9)

Romans (Chapters 1,2,6,7!,8,10,13)

I Corinthians (Chapters 4,6,7 wrote by Paul,10,11,13,15)

II Corinthians (Chapters 1,3,4,6★,9,10,11,12,13)

Galatians (Chapters 3,4)

Ephesians (Chapter 5)

Philippians (Chapter 2)

Colossians (Chapter 1)

I Thessalonians (Chapter 4)

I Timothy (Chapters 2,3,4,5,6 Paul Words)

II Timothy (Chapter 4)

Titus (Chapters 2,3)

Hebrews (Chapters 1,6,10,11)

James (Chapters 1,3,5)

I Peter (Chapter 2)

I John (Chapters 2,3,4)

Revelation (Chapters 4,5,14,20)

The Old Testament

GENESIS – (1:3-4) (6:3) (8:21-22 pink) (9:1-10★,11-16 pink,17-19 blue)

(12:2-3) (13:8) (15:1) (19:7 green) (28:3,16-17★★,21 pink,22★★) (32:12,20)

(33:8★) (35:11) (45:5★★,7-8) (46:3-4) (48:4,18-19 green)

(49:14-15★) (50:17 pink,20★★,21)

EXODUS – (2:25★pink) (3:14) (4:11) (14:14) (15:2-3,18 green,26)

(16:8★★) (18:11) (19:5 blue) (20:3-17 The Ten Commandments)

(21:12 green,14-15 green,17,23-25★★) (22:21★,28★,31★★)

(23:2★★,13★,24-25,30 blue,32-33) (32:32 MW,33-34 GW) (33:5,13 MW,14-15 GW)

(34:10★,14 green,29-30★ no vagueness) (35:2-5 MW,8 pink)

LEVITICUS – (3:17★) (8:33-35★✔correct) (9:7 pink✔) (10:9★)

(11:43-45 GW,46-47) (16:29,31,34 ★) (18:22)

(19:2★,3-4,11-12,15-18,28★★,30-33,34 pink,35-36 blue,37)

(20:7-8,24-26★) (21:4 pink) (22:21 blue,32 pink)

(25:8★★,17★★) (26:1 green,2 blue,13)

NUMBERS – (6:24-26) (12:3 patient/mild) (14:9,11-12,19 pink)

(15:30 blue) (23:19-20 blue,22) (24:9 blue,17 blue)

(25:12-13★) (30:2★) (35:34 green)

The Old Testament

DEUTERONOMY – (1:17 green,21★★) (3:24-25) (4:9★,39-40★)

(5:12★,16★,21★,27,31,33 ★) (6:18-19) (7:2,6★,9-10,21,26 ★★)

(8:5★★,10★★,18★★) (9:13-14★) (10:14 blue,16-22)

(11:16★★,18-21★★,26-28★) (13:18 blue) (14:2-3) (15:6★★,7-11★)

(16:20★★,22★★) (17:20★★) (18:10-13) (19:9 pink) (20:1,4★★) (21:8-10)

(22:5★★,6-7) (24:5,16 green) (25:13-15) (26:16-19★)

(28:1-2★,12-14★,20 green,47 blue) (30:15-16 blue✔,19 blue) (31:8★)

(32:35 greenGW,39-40 blue) (33:23-24 green)

JOSHUA – (1:5-7★★,8-9★,17-18★★)

(3:5★★✔daily,7★) (14:11) (24:14★★,15,23★★)

JUDGES – (6:23 pink) (8:2★★,5★★) (9:1-2) (18:5-6 ★★)

RUTH – (2:12 green)

I SAMUEL – (2:2-3 green,6-7,8-10★★,30★★) (3:13★) (7:3★) (8:7-9)

(10:24 pink,27 pink) (12:23 pink,24★) (14:27★★) (15:23 green) (16:7,23 blue)

(18:14) (21:15★blue) (22:23 green) (23:21★pink) (25:6 pink) (26:24★) (30:12)

II SAMUEL – (3:18★,33-34 green★,39 green) (6:14-22!)

(7:22★★,29) (10:12 ✔★★) (19:7✗) (22:1-51★ Davids psalm of thanksgiving)

(23:3-4★) (24:14★★)

I KINGS – (2:1-3★) (3:8-14★) (8:39★,50 pink,57 blue,60 blue,61★★)

(9:4-9) (10:9★★) (11:38★★) (12:7 omw)

II KINGS – (6:16-23★) (17:35-39,40-41 green)

(19:19 blue,34 green) (20:1-11★ life) (22:19-20 pink)

I CHRONICLES – (4:10★★)

(16:8-12,14 blue,15,23★,24 blue,25,27-29 ★34-36)

(17:27★) (19:13★) (21:12-14) (22:8★,9-10 green,11-16,19)

(23:30★★) (28:7-10,20) (29:1★★,3,10-20★ King Davids great prayer)

II CHRONICLES – (1:10-12) (2:4,5★★,9★) (6:40 blue,42 pink)

(7:14 blue) (9:8 blue✔) (10:7 ⊘ pink omw) (12:6★ pink★)

(13:11,12 green) (15:7★,12-15★★) (16:9 green) (19:7 green)

(20:17) (26:5★★) (29:5,11) (30:7★★,8,9 ★★) (32:7-8★★)

The Old Testament

EZRA – (4:22 green) (6:10 green) (10:4★★,11)

NEHEMIAH – (5:19 pink) (9:5-6 blue,33★★) (13:2 pink)

ESTHER – (8:6)

JOB – (1:22) (2:10★) (4:8 green) (5:17★★) (8:6-9★,20★) (11:14-20★)

(12:10 green) (13:15 blue,19 blue) (15:20 green) (16:19 blue) (17:9★★)

(19:21 blue) (22:21-28★) (25:5) (27:3-4✔, 6★★) (28:28★★) (31:28-30)

(33:3-4,8-9,12-13 blue★,26★★,31-33★) (36:5 pink,6-7 green,11★★,21 green★ focus)

(37:14★★) (40:10-14 pink) (42:10 green)

The Old Testament

PSALMS – (1:1-3) (4:3★✔,4★★) (5:3 blue,4-5,8 blue,11★)

(7:6-7 green,8-9★★IndignationArise,17★★) (9:1★★) (10:17-18★★) (11:7★★)

(16:8-11) (17:7 pink,15★★) (18:3 pink) (19:1 blue,8-11★,14★) (20:3-4★★)

(21:13 pink) (23:1★★,4,6 pink) (24:1★★,7-9 pink) (25:2 green) (26:3 pink,11)

(27:1★,9★,14★★) (28:7★★) (29:2★★,3 blue) (30:1-3,12)

(31:1,3★★,5-6★,15 green,16★★,21,24★) (32:5-6 green durst,8★✔)

(34:1 blue,13-14★★✔) (35:9★✔,13 green,18,28★)

(37:1-2 green,4-5★,7-8 green,11 green,23★,27 green) (41:1-3) (44:8★★)

(45:17 purple) (46:10 blue) (47:1★,7) (49:7 green) (51:8 pink,10★★,12-13★✔)

(55:17 blue,22-23★) (57:7-8 blue) (59:16-17★★) (62:3,8★,10) (63:3 pink)

(66:4,20) (68:34 blue) (71:1★★,14★★,18★★) (74:22 green) (75:5-7★★)

(76:11-12 green) (77:7-9 pink,10-12 green) (80:1-7★,19★★) (81:1★,9-10★)

(84:12) (85:1-8★★✔Forgiveness/Mercy) (86:10,12★) (90:12★,14★)

(91:11,16 pink) (92:1-2★,10 pink) (96:7★✔) (100:3★★) (101:2-3★★✔) (103:8 pink)

(104:15,33-34) (105:4 blue,14-15★★) (108:1-3★) (109:26-27★★) (110:1★)

(112:7 green) (113:2-3★✔) (115:16 blue,18 blue★) (116:5★,18) (118:6,8-9,17,24,26★★)

(119:15-16★★,45-46 green,62★,68★,80★★,157 pink,164 blue,165 pink)

(120:2 blue,7 blue) (121:1 green,7,8 blue) (122:6-9 pink) (125:4 pink) (126:5 blue)

(129:8★) (133:1★★) (135:3) (140:11 green) (142:7★★) (143:10★★)

(144:14-15★★ no complaining) (145:2 pink,17★★) (147:1★★,10-11) (149:5★★)

PROVERBS – (1:8-9★★) (3:11★★) (4:3-4 pink,7-9★★,23-26★) (5:15,18-19 pink)

(6:5★,16-23★★,25★★,32★) (8:8★,13★ angerlanguage,19★rest,35 green)

(9:6,11-12 green) (10:1 pink,4 green,10,12,18) (11:1-2★,12 green,17★,27-31)

(12:25 goodwords) (13:24-25) (14:7,13,29-31 pink,35★) (15:3 blue,27,30★33)

(16:3★★,7 pink,12-14★★,19-20★★,24 pink) (17:1★,22★,25,28★) (18:7,21 green)

(19:1,8,13,18 ★) (20:13★,22 green,29★) (21:4★,9,19,21,29,31)

(22:1 pink,4★★,6 pink,9 pink,15★,24-26★29 pink) (23:7★,13-14,15-17★★,26★★)

(24:13★,15,16 blue,17-19★★,29 green) (25:3★★,21 ★★) (26:27 green)

(27:1 blue,2,7 blue,11 blue) (28:9★,14★)

(29:15★,17-18★,23★★) (30:32) (31:4-7,10-12)

ECCLESIASTES – (1:4,18) (4:9-11) (5:4★,5,12★,15)

(7:1 pink,3★★,5,8★★,16-17) (9:4★) (10:2,20 green)

(11:7★✔,9-10 green) (12:12,14★★)

SONG OF SOLOMON – (1:13 pink) (8:3 pink,6 pink,14 pink)

ISAIAH – (1:16 blue✔,19) (2:5★✔) (3:10-12) (5:11,15) (6:5) (7:15)

(8:13★✔) (9:6-7 green) (12:6★★) (14:3-15) (18:4 blue) (24:15★★)

(26:3-4★,20-21★) (29:15 green) (30:1-2★★,18★★,26★★,29★★) (31:1★★,6 green)

(32:20 blue) (33:15-16★,22★★) (34:16-17) (35:1-10) (37:28-29 blue)

(38:5★,19 blue) (40:1★★,3 green,8-9 blue,20★,28-30★,31 blue) (42:13-14)

(43:1-2★★,18-19✔★★,23-24★) (44:6) (45:7,13★,22 blue,23 green)

(46:3-5 pinkGW,8★★"show MAN") (48:22) (49:9★) (50:6-8 green)

(51:7,9-11 blue,12,18) (54:4★★,11,17★★) (55:5 green,7-9★) (56:1-2★★)

(57:2,15-16★,19★,21) (58:4-8★,10★★,13-14★) (59:2★,17-18 green) (60:15,19-20)

(61:1-2 green,10) (62:10 blue) (65:16-18★,23★★) (66:4-5,10-14 The New Jerusalem)

JEREMIAH – (1:7-8★★,17★,19 blue) (2:32★★) (3:20) (4:14★★) (5:5★)

(6:15-16★) (9:23-24★) (10:2★★,5,19 blue✔,24) (13:15★★,18★,25-26 ★)

(14:7-10,21 pink) (15:15★) (16:17 blue) (17:5★,7★,10★★,13-14★,21-22 green)

(21:13 green) (23:24 blue) (25:30★★) (29:7-9★★,12-13★) (30:17 green)

(31:7 pink,30) (32:17★★,19★★,27★★,33,37-42) (39:18 green) (45:5 green)

(47:6★) (49:15-16,31★,34-39 Ē´lam) (50:6 green,31 blue) (52:31-34)

The Old Testament

LAMENTATIONS – (3:25 pink,36,41 pink,58-66) (5:1-3 green)

EZEKIEL -   (2:6) (12:5-6★,18★★) (17:24 green) (18:4-9★,20,31-32)

  (22:14-16) (28:1-9) (33:11★) (36:22-23★★,24-30★) (43:12★,26-27[★])

  (44:9) (45:9 green,10★★✓) (46:13 blue/make intercession)

DANIEL – (4:27accepted,37abase pride) (5:10★★,20 blue)

  (10:2-3,19 blue✔) (12:3 blue)

HOSEA – (4:11★★) (6:1-2★★,6★★) (10:12★) (12:6★★)

JOEL – (2:12-15 green,21★,27 green,31) (3:10 green)

AMOS – (5:14★★) (6:6★★) (9:2)

OBADIAH – (1:1-15★)

MICAH – (6:1 green,8★★) (7:6-7,18-20 pink)

HABAKKUK – (1:12-13 blue) (2:1-4★★) (3:12 green,13-19 pink)

ZEPHANIAH – (1:14-18 pink) (2:11) (3:15 blue✔)

HAGGAI – (2:4★)

ZECHARIAH – (1:4 green) (3:8 green) (6:12-13 green)

(7:9-10 green,14 green) (8:16-17 green,23 green) (10:12 green) (12:10 green)

MALACHI – (1:11★) (2:10 pink) (3:8,10★) (4:2 blue,5-6)

END OF THE
OLD TESTAMENT

THE NEW TESTAMENT

ST. MATTHEW – (4:10ᴊᴡ★) (5:16ᴊᴡ, 39ᴊᴡ, 44ᴊᴡ, 48ᴊᴡ)

(6:6-18ᴊᴡ, 22ᴊᴡ, 24-25ᴊᴡ, 27ᴊᴡ, 33ᴊᴡ) (7:1-2ᴊᴡ, 5ᴊᴡ, 7-8ᴊᴡ, 12ᴊᴡ)

(8:1-4ᴊᴡ, 21-22ᴊᴡ) (9:13ᴊᴡ) (11:6ᴊᴡ, 8ᴊᴡ, 28-30ᴊᴡ)

(12:25ᴊᴡ, 33ᴊᴡ, 36-37ᴊᴡ, 40ᴊᴡ, 50ᴊᴡ) (13:57ᴊᴡ) (15:8-9ᴊᴡ)

(16:23-28ᴊᴡ) (17:15-17ᴊᴡ, 18, 20ᴊᴡ) (18:1-5ᴊᴡ, 10ᴊᴡ, 19-22ᴊᴡ, 35ᴊᴡ)

(19:5-9ᴊᴡ, 17ᴊᴡ, 21ᴊᴡ, 26ᴊᴡ, 29-30ᴊᴡ) (20:1-16ᴊᴡ Hired Labourers)

(21:13ᴊᴡ, 21-22ᴊᴡ, 28-32ᴊᴡ) (22:32ᴊᴡ, 37-40ᴊᴡ, 44ᴊᴡ) (23:9-12ᴊᴡ, 39ᴊᴡ)

(25:14-46ᴊᴡ) (26:23-24ᴊᴡ, 38-41ᴊᴡ, 52ᴊᴡ, 64ᴊᴡ) (28:19-20ᴊᴡ)

ST. MARK – (3:24-25ᴊᴡ, 28-29ᴊᴡ, 35ᴊᴡ) (4:20ᴊᴡ, 24ᴊᴡ, 30-32ᴊᴡ)

(6:4ᴊᴡ, 12-13) (7:27ᴊᴡ) (8:31, 34-38ᴊᴡ) (9:37ᴊᴡ, 50ᴊᴡ) (10:11-12ᴊᴡ!,18ᴊᴡ, 44ᴊᴡ)

(11:23-26ᴊᴡ) (13:11-13ᴊᴡ, 31-37ᴊᴡ) (14:38ᴊᴡ, 62ᴊᴡ) (16:15-18ᴊᴡ, 19-20)

ST. LUKE – (1:37★,68-79★) (2:14 pink) (3:14★,23) (4:1-13 Satan tempts Jesus)

(5:20-26 forgiven, 32✓jw) (6:19 pink⬤, 20-49jw) (7:23jw) (9:56jw, 58-62jw)

(10:2-5jw, 16jw, 17 green,19-20jw, 24jw, 41-42jw)

(11:9-10jw, 13jw, 17jw, 34-36jw, 39jw) (12:5jw, 22-23jw, 29-31jw, 59jw)

(14:11-14jw, 26jw?, 27-32jw, 33jw?, 34-35jw) (15:7jw) (16:13jw, 18jw!) (17:1-4jw)

(18:1, 3jw, 10-14jw) (19:38-39, 40jw, 41, 42-44jw, 45, 46jw, 47-48) (20:34-38jw!)

(21:14-19jw, 26-28jw, 34-36jw) (22:19-20jw, 64-65 blue 4 L Sake, 69jw)

(23:28jw, 34jw) (24:38-39jw ME, 45, 46-49jw, 50-53 be proper and do the will of God)

ST. JOHN – (1:51jw) (3:3jw, 5-8jw, 16-21jw, 31-36) (4:24jw, 34-37jw)

(5:42jw Have the Love of God in you)

(6:14-15green★ Humility★, 35jw, 38-40jw, 47jw, 51jw, 53jw, 56jw)

(7:19★jw, 24jw, 37-38jw, 39★★)

(8:12jw, 14-16jw, 23jw, 28-29jw, 31-32jw, 34-38jw, 42jw, 49-51jw, 54-55jw)

(9:4-5jw) (10:1-11jw, 17-18jw, 27-30jw, 34-38!)

(11:9-10jw, 25-26jw, 35jw) (12:23-32★jw, 35-36jw, 44-47jw)

(13:14-17jw, 34-35jw) (14:1-4jw, 6-7★jw, 13-21jw, 23jw, 27-29jw)

(15:4-9jw★, 18jw) (16:1jw, 20jw, 22-24jw, 33jw)

(17:9-10jw, 15-16jw, 21-23★jw) (20:23jw-forgive L.I.G., 29jw) (21:15-18jw)

The New Testament

ACTS – (2:20, 38★★,40-41★★) (4:30-33 pink) (5:29★,32★) (6:4★*)

(7:51,55-56 blue) (8:32-35,36-37★★) (10:34-35★★,36 pink,38-43)

(11:16ᴊᴡ,24★) (13:10-11) (14:22 blue) (15:29★★) (16:31 green) (17:23-31★)

(20:22-24 green,25-32,33★★,35 ᴘᴡ-ᴊᴡ) (24:14-15★,16★★) (26:18*ᴊᴡ,20★)

ROMANS – (1:7-9 blue,15-17 blue) (2:1 green,6-7★,25-29★) (3:10-19*)

(4:19-22) (5:3-5★★,19-21★★) (6:14★★) (8:6,11★,13,18★★,28★,31-33★,38-39★★)

(9:25-26, 28, 32-33★★) (10:1★, 9, 11★, 12★★,17) (11:6★★ No Work,22 blue)

(12:1-3 blue,8★★be nice,9-21★★) (13:1-2 green,8★, 12-14★★)

(14:3,6-10,13★17-18★,19 blue,20-22) (15:3,7 pink,13★,29-33 pink)

(16:16 pink,17,19-20 green,24 pink,27 green)

I CORINTHIANS – (1:3,9 pink,20,25,27-28★★,31) (2:5★★)

(3:6-9★★,10★,16-17 green,21★★) (4:4-6★,10★★,19-21★) (5:6-8,13★green)

(6:19,20 pink) (7:1-5★,19,29,31,37) (8:6 green) (9:24-27)

(10:10★,12★★,14★,31-33 pink)

(11:3 green,7 green,9, 13-17!, 24-25ᴊᵂ, 27-29 pink,31-32 green)

(12:3 blue Jesus is the Lord, 5 blue, 23-24, 26★) (13:2-7,11★,13 pink)

(14:1 pink,15★,20 green,33 pink,38-39 green,40 blue)

(15:10★★,25-26★ no enemies,30-32 green,33-34,51-52,58★★) (16:13★★,14 pink,20 pink)

II CORINTHIANS – (1:6-7 pink,12★,20 blue★) (2:9-11★★)

(3:17 green) (4:15-18★★★) (5:7-8★,10 green,15★,17 blue,18-21★) (6:1-4★★)

(7:1 pink,4★,9-11) (8:9,10 blue,11★★,12★,24★) (9:6-7★★)

(10:7 pink,12★★,17★★) (12:9ᴊᵂ,10 pink,11-12) (13:5-7★,11-14 pink)

GALATIANS – (1:3-5 pink) (2:6-8,14-21) (3:13 green) (4:18 green)

(5:1 green,4★,6★,13-14 pink,16★★,18★,22-26★★)

(6:3-4 green,7⊘8, 9✓blue,14★,17✓blue)

EPHESIANS – (1:3-4 pink,15-16 pink,18 pink,22-23 green)

(2:7-9 pink,19,20-22 green) (3:17 pink,21 blue)

(4:1-2 green,3 pink,13-15★,17-18★,24★★,26★,29★,30 blue Don't Grieve,31★,32★★)

(5:1-2 pink,8★★,11 green,14★★,15-17★,19 pink,20 blue) (6:1-4 pink,8,10-17 green)

PHILIPPIANS – (1:20-21★★,28-29★★) (2:3 blue,14)

(3:2,13-14★★,20-21 blue) (4:4-5 blue,11-12,13 green,19,21 pink)

COLOSSIANS – (1:10 pink,16-17★)

(3:1,2 pink,8,12-16 pink,17 green,20 pink,21,23-24 pink,25) (4:2-3★,5,6 pink)

I THESSALONIANS – (2:12★★) (3:12-13 pink)

(4:7 green,11-13★) (5:6 green,8 green,11,15 green,16★★,17,18 pink,22★★,25)

II THESSALONIANS – (2:8 green,17 blue) (3:6★,9-15★)

I TIMOTHY – (2:8★,11-13) (4:8 green,16★★)

(5:1-2★,21★,22★★) (6:6★★,7-8★,10 green,12 green,17 green,18)

II TIMOTHY – (1:3 pink,6-9★★)

(2:1★★,3★★,15 blue,16★★,23★★) (3:12-17★) (4:5★★,6-8,9 blue)

TITUS – (2:12★★) (3:2★★)

HEBREWS – (3:4) (6:12 green) (7:2★,22 green) (8:10 green,12 pink)

(9:28) (10:22-23★★,24 pink,30 green,31-39★) (11:6 blue)

(12:1★,5-7★,12-14★) (13:1-2 pink,3★,5,8 blue,9,15,16 ★★,21 green)

JAMES – (1:22-25★★) (2:8★★,19★★,20 green,26 green)

(4:4,6★★,7-12★,14-17★★) (5:7-9★,12,13★★,16★)

I PETER – (1:13-16,23★★[★]) (2:1 green,15-17 green,22-25★)

  (3:3-4★,8 pink,9-10★,12,14,17★★) (4:1-2★,8-9 pink,11★★,14-16)

  (5:5★,6-8 pink,10-11 pink,14 pink)

II PETER – (1:5-10★) (2:11-12,21-22) (3:7-8★,18★★)

I JOHN – (1:5★) (3:4 the Mosaic law, 18★★ Good Deeds, 22★★) (5:4-13★★,21)

II JOHN – (1:7-8)

III JOHN – (1:2★★,4-6 pink A Godly Sort,11★★,14★★⊘)

JUDE – (1:8-15★,21 pink,24-25★)

REVELATION – (1:3★★,11ᴊᴡ, 17-18ᴊᴡ) (2:4-7ᴊᴡ, 10ᴊᴡ, 25-29ᴊᴡ)

  (3:7-12ᴊᴡ, 19ᴊᴡ, 21ᴊᴡ) (7:12 pink) (13:18!) (14:13) (15:3 pink,4★)

  (21:6, 16-27 Heaven, 240 feet wall height: 1500 miles long, breadth, & height)

  (22:11, 12-13ᴊᴡ, 14-15 green,16ᴊᴡ, 17)

END OF THE
NEW TESTAMENT

This Section Is With All The Scripture I've Selected, Divided, And Linked Into Fifty-Seven Different Groups, Named, Characterized To Help

1. Love & Charity
2. Fear
3. Healing
4. Happiness
5. Holy Ghost
6. Food & Drink
7. Chasten
8. God The Maker
9. Despising
10. Falsehood
11. Jesus
12. Clean & Unclean
13. Obedience
14. Being Good
15. Being Proud
16. The Sabbath
17. Blessings
18. Prayer
19. Idols

20. Individuals
21. Grace & Mercy
22. Praise & Thanks
23. Singing
24. Evildoers
25. Sanctification
26. Protection
27. Wisdom
28. Faith
29. Righteous Anger
30. Forgiveness
31. Worry
32. Covet
33. Sorrow
34. Pity
35. Speaking Nice
36. Living Life
37. Liberty
38. Enemies

39. The Light
40. Trusting God
41. Being Strong
42. Judging
43. Being Humble
44. Offerings
45. Vainglory
46. Peace
47. Weeping
48. Helping
49. Rest & Patience
50. Wrath
51. Followers
52. Moving Forward
53. Fasting
54. Strife
55. Honor & Respect
56. Glory
57. Comfort

Leviticus (19:34 pink) --- Deuteronomy (19:9 pink) (21:8-10)

I Samuel (10:24 pink) --- II Chronicles (6:42 pink)

Nehemiah (5:19 pink) --- Psalms (17:7 pink, 15★★) (26:3 pink)

Psalms (31:21) (63:3 pink) (77:7-9 pink, 10-12 green) (92:2★) (133:1★★)

Proverbs (8:35 green) (10:12) (16:7 pink, 24 pink) (22:1 pink, 6 pink, 9 pink)

Song of Solomon (1:13 pink) (8:14 pink) --- Isaiah (45:13★)

Jeremiah (14:21 pink) --- Ezekiel (46:13 blue) --- Micah (6:8★★)

Micah (7:18-20 pink)   END OF OLD TESTAMENT

St. Matthew (5:44JW) (7:12JW) (22:37-40JW)

St. Luke (2:14 pink) (9:56JW) --- St. John (5:42JW Have the Love of God in you)

St. John (8:42JW) (13:34-35JW) (14:21JW, 23JW) (15:9JW) (21:15-18JW)

Acts (24:16★★) (26:18★JW) --- Romans (1:9 blue) (6:14★★) (9:25-26,28)

Romans (12:9-21★★) (13:8★) (14:19 blue) (15:7 pink, 29-30 pink, 32 pink)

Romans (16:16 pink) --- I Corinthians (4:19-21★) (13:2-7,13 pink)

I Corinthians (14:1 pink, 33 pink) (16:14 pink, 20 pink)

II Corinthians (8:24★) (13:11-14 pink) --- Galatians (5:13-14 pink)

Ephesians (1:15-16 pink, 18 pink) (3:17 pink) (4:32 ★★) (5:1-2 pink)

Philippians (4:21 pink) --- Colossians (3:12-14 pink)

I Thessalonians (3:12-13 pink) --- I Timothy (4:8 green, 16★★)

Titus (3:2★★) --- Hebrews (10:24 pink) (13:1-2 pink, 3★)

TURN TO NEXT PAGE ONE ⟹

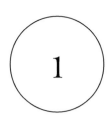

I PETER (2:17 green) (3:8 pink,9-10★) (4:8-9 pink) (5:5★,14 pink)

I JOHN (3:18★★ Good Deeds)

III JOHN (1:4-6 pink A Godly Sort)

Jude (1:21 pink)

FEAR

Numbers (14:9)

Deuteronomy (1:21★★) (7:21) (31:8★)

II Kings (6:16)

II Chronicles (32:7-8★★)

Psalms (27:1★)

Isaiah (51:7,12) (54:4★★)

Jeremiah (1:7-8★★,17★)

Ezekiel (2:6)

Joel (2:21★)

Malachi (4:2 blue)

END OF OLD TESTAMENT

St. Luke (12:5ᴊᴡ)

I Peter (3:14)

HEALING

II Kings (20:1-11★ life)

Psalms (27:14★★) (30:2-3) (31:24★) (46:10 blue) (51:8 pink)

Proverbs (16:24 pink)

Isaiah (30:15★★) (40:31 blue) (57:19★)

Jeremiah (30:17 green)

Hosea (6:1-2★★)

Malachi (4:2 blue)

    END OF OLD TESTAMENT

Acts (4:30 pink)

Romans (8:11★)

Hebrews (12:12-14★)

HAPPINESS

Deuteronomy (28:47 blue)

I Samuel (16:23 blue)

Job (5:17★★) (36:11★★)

Psalms (5:11★) (51:8 pink, 12-13★✔)

Psalms (118:24) (126:5 blue) (144:14-15★★ no complaining)

Psalms (149:5★★)

Proverbs (14:13) (16:20★★) (17:22★★)

Proverbs (31:10-12)

Isaiah (30:29★★)

Joel (2:21★)

   END OF OLD TESTAMENT

Romans (15:29-30 pink,32 pink)

Philippians (4:4-5 blue)

I Thessalonians (5:16★★)

I Peter (3:14)

St. Luke (11:13 jw)

St. John (4:24 jw) (7:39★★)

Acts (2:38★★,40-41★★) (4:31-32 pink) (5:32★) (7:51,55-56 blue)

Acts (10:38-43★) (11:16 jw,24 ★) (20:22-24 green,25-32)

Romans (5:5★★) (15:13★)

I Corinthians (6:19) (12:3 blue Jesus is the Lord)

Galatians (5:16★★,22-26★★)

Ephesians (4:30 blue Don't Grieve)

END OF NEW TESTAMENT

Leviticus (3:17★) (10:9★)

Deuteronomy (8:10★★)

I Samuel (30:12)

Proverbs (5:15) (8:19★ rest) (31:4-7)

Isaiah (7:15)

Ezekiel (12:18★★)

END OF OLD TESTAMENT

St. Matthew (6:25ᴊᴡ, 31ᴊᴡ)

St. Mark (7:27ᴊᴡ)

St. Luke (22:19-20ᴊᴡ)

Romans (14:3)

I Corinthians (11:24-25ᴊᴡ, 27-29 pink)

CHASTEN

Deuteronomy (8:5★★)

I Chronicles (21:12-14)

Job (1:22) (5:17★★) (13:15 blue)

Psalms (37:23★)

Proverbs (3:11★★) (13:24) (19:18★) (22:15★) (23:13-14) (29:15★,17★)

END OF OLD TESTAMENT

II Corinthians (12:10 pink,11-12)

II Timothy (2:3★★)

Hebrews (12:5-7★)

I Peter (3:14)

Revelation (3:19ᴊᴡ)

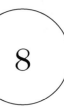

Genesis (6:3) (8:21-22 pink) (9:1-10★,11-16 pink,17-19 blue)

Genesis (12:2-3 purple) (15:1) (28:16-17★★) (32:12,20) (35:11)

Genesis (45:7-8 purple) (48:4 purple,18-19 green) (50:20★★)

Exodus (3:14) (4:11) (15:3) (20:3-17 The Ten Commandments)

Exodus (21:17 purple) (33:5 purple,13 pink,14-15 purple) (34:10★)

Exodus (35:2-4 purple) --- Leviticus (19:3,18,28★★,31,33) (26:13)

Numbers (23:19-20 blue,22) (24:17 blue)

Deuteronomy (7:9-10) (10:14 blue,16-22) (32:35 green,39-40 blue)

Joshua (3:7★) --- I Samuel (2:2 green,6-7)

II Samuel (3:18★) (7:22★★)

I Chronicles (16:14 blue) (22:8★,9-10 green,11-16,19)

II Chronicles (16:9 green) --- Job (12:10 green) (36:6-7 green)

Psalms (20:4★★) (24:1★★) (76:12 green) (86:10) (100:3★★) (115:16 blue)

Proverbs (15:3 blue) --- Ecclesiastes (12:14★★)

Isaiah (9:6-7 green) (14:3-15) (30:26★★) (40:3 green,8-9 blue,28-30★)

Isaiah (44:6) (45:7,22 blue,23 green) (46:3-5 pink) (55:8-9★)

Isaiah (56:1-2★★) --- Jeremiah (16:17 blue) (23:24 blue) (25:30★★)

Jeremiah (32:17★★,19★★,27★★,37-42) (49:34-39 Ē′lam)

Ezekiel (17:24 green) (18:4-9★,20) (36:22-23★★,24-30★)

Joel (2:27 green,31) --- Amos (9:2) --- Obadiah (1:1-15)

Zephaniah (1:14-18 pink) (2:11) (3:15 blue) TURN TO NEXT PAGE EIGHT

Zechariah (3:8 green) (6:12-13 green) (7:9-10 green, 14 green) (8:23 green)

Zechariah (10:12 green) (12:10 green) --- Malachi (1:11★) (4:5)

END OF OLD TESTAMENT

St. Matthew (22:32) --- St. Mark (8:31)

St. Luke (1:68-79★) (20:38ᴊᴡ) --- St. John (3:31-36)

Acts (2:20) (17:23-31★)

Romans (8:11★,28★,31-33★) (14:17-18★,20-22)

I Corinthians (1:9 pink,27-28★★) (8:6 green) (12:5 blue,23-24)

II Corinthians (5:18-21★) --- Galatians (4:18 green)

Ephesians (1:22-23 green) (2:19,20-22 green)

Colossians (1:16-17★) --- II Thessalonians (2:8 green)

II Timothy (1:7-9★★) --- Hebrews (3:4) (7:22 green)

Hebrews (8:10 green,12 pink) (10:30 green,31-39★) (11:6 blue)

James (2:8★★,19★★) --- I Peter (3:12) --- I John (1:5★)

Jude (1:24-25★)

Revelation (21:6,16-27 Heaven, 240 feet wall height:
                1500 miles long, breadth, & height)

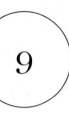

Exodus (16:8★★)

Leviticus (19:17)

Numbers (35:34 green)

Deuteronomy (7:26★★)

Job (5:17★★) (27:4✔) (36:5 pink)

Psalms (34:13-14★★) (62:3) (120:2 blue)

Proverbs (3:11★★) (9:11-12 green) (10:18)

Ecclesiastes (10:20 green)

END OF OLD TESTAMENT

Ephesians (4:29★,31★)

I Peter (2:1 green) (3:10★)

FALSEHOOD

Leviticus (19:11-12)

II Chronicles (13:12 green)

Proverbs (6:16-19★★) (10:18)

Jeremiah (13:25-26★) (29:8-9★★)

Ezekiel (28:1-9)

END OF OLD TESTAMENT

Romans (3:10-19★)

St. Matthew (4:10jw★) (6:27jw) (8:21-22jw) (11:8jw)

St. Matthew (12:25jw,40jw,50jw) (13:57jw) (15:8-9jw) (16:23-28jw)

St. Matthew (17:15,16-18jw,20jw) (18:1-5jw,10jw,19-22jw,35jw)

St. Matthew (19:5-9jw,17jw,21jw,26jw,29-30jw)

St. Matthew (20:1-16jw Hired Labourers) (21:13jw,21-22jw,28-32jw)

St. Matthew (22:32jw,37-40jw,44jw) (23:9-12jw,39jw) (25:14-46jw)

St. Matthew (26:23-24jw,38-41jw,52jw,64jw) (28:19-20jw)

St. Mark (3:24-25jw,28-29jw,35jw) (4:20jw,24jw,30-32jw) (6:4jw)

St. Mark (8:34-38jw) (9:37jw,50jw) (10:11-12jw!,18jw,44jw)

St. Mark (13:11-13jw,31-37jw) (14:38jw,62jw) (16:15-18jw,19-20)

St. Luke (3:23) (4:1-13 Satan tempts Jesus) (5:20-26 forgiven,32jw✓) (6:20-49jw)

St. Luke (7:23jw) (9:56jw,58-62jw) (10:2-5jw,16jw,19-20jw, 24jw,41-42jw)

St. Luke (11:9-10jw,13jw,17jw,34-36jw,39jw) (12:5jw,22-23jw,29-31jw,59jw)

St. Luke (14:11-14jw,26jw?,27-32jw,33jw?,34-35jw) (15:7jw) (16:13jw,18jw!)

St. Luke (17:1-4jw) (18:3jw,10-14jw) (19:38-39,40jw,41,42-44jw,45,46jw,47-48)

St. Luke (20:34-38jw!) (21:14-19jw,26-28jw,34-36jw) (22:19-20jw,69jw)

St. Luke (24:38-39jw,45,46-49jw,50-53 be proper and do the will of God)

St. John (1:51jw) (3:3jw,5-8jw,16-21jw) (4:24jw,34jw)

St. John (5:42jw Have the Love of God in you)

St. John (6:14-15green★Humility★,35jw,38-40jw,47jw,51jw,53jw,56jw)

TURN TO NEXT PAGE ELEVEN ➡

St. John (7:19★ᴊᴡ,37-38ᴊᴡ,39★★)

St. John (8:12ᴊᴡ,23ᴊᴡ,28-29ᴊᴡ,31-32ᴊᴡ,34-38ᴊᴡ,42ᴊᴡ,49ᴊᴡ,54-55ᴊᴡ)

St. John (10:1-11ᴊᴡ,17-18ᴊᴡ,27-30ᴊᴡ,34-38!) (11:25-26ᴊᴡ)

St. John (12:23-32★ᴊᴡ,44-47ᴊᴡ) (13:14-17ᴊᴡ)

St. John (14:1-4ᴊᴡ,6-7★ᴊᴡ,17-21ᴊᴡ,23ᴊᴡ,27-29ᴊᴡ) (15:4-8ᴊᴡ★,18ᴊᴡ)

St. John (16:1ᴊᴡ,20ᴊᴡ,22-24ᴊᴡ,33ᴊᴡ) (17:21-23★ᴊᴡ) (21:15-18ᴊᴡ)

Acts (10:38-43★) --- I Corinthians (11:24-25ᴊᴡ)

II Corinthians (5:15★) --- Hebrews (9:28) (13:8 blue)

I Peter (2:22-25★) --- Revelation (1:11ᴊᴡ,17-18ᴊᴡ) (2:4-7ᴊᴡ,10ᴊᴡ,25-29ᴊᴡ)

Revelation (3:7-12ᴊᴡ,19ᴊᴡ,21ᴊᴡ) (22:12-13ᴊᴡ,16ᴊᴡ)

END OF NEW TESTAMENT

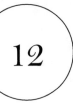

Leviticus (11:43-45 purple,46-47 pink) (18:22) (20:24-26★)

Deuteronomy (7:2)

II Chronicles (19:7 green)

Ezra (10:11)

Job (17:9★★) (33:8-9)

Psalms (1:1-3) (5:4-5) (51:10★★)

Proverbs (14:7)

Isaiah (6:5)

Ezekiel (8:31-32) (44:9)

ENDOF OLD TESTAMENT

II Corinthians (7:1 pink)

Exodus (19:5 blue)

Leviticus (19:37)

Deuteronomy (5:27,31) (28:1-2★,12-14★)

Joshua (1:8★,17-18★★)

I Kings (3:14★) (11:38★★)

I Chronicles (28:7-10)

II Chronicles (29:11)

Job (36:11★★)

Psalms (119:15-16★★,157 pink)

Proverbs (4:3-4 pink) (23:26★★)

Isaiah (1:19)

END OF OLD TESTAMENT

Acts (5:29★,32★)

I Corinthians (15:58 ★★)

Ephesians (6:1-4 pink)

Colossians (3:20 pink)

I Peter (1:13-16)

Genesis (19:7 green) --- Exodus (15:26) (23:2★★)

Deuteronomy (3:24-25) (6:18-19) (13:18 blue) 16:20★★) (18:13)

Deuteronomy (19:9 pink) (26:16-19★) --- I Samuel (18:14)

II Samuel (10:12★★✓) --- I Kings (8:61★★) (9:4-9)

I Chronicles (19:13★) --- Nehemiah (5:19 pink) (9:33★★)

Job (8:6-9★) (17:9★★) (33:3,12-13 blue*,31-33★) (36:21 green* focus)

Psalms (1:1-3) (5:8 blue) (19:14★) (23:6 pink) (34:13-14★★)

Psalms (37:27 green) (91:16 pink) (101:2-3★★) (119:68★) (120:2 blue)

Psalms (125:4 pink) --- Proverbs (21:21) (22:1 pink,6 pink,9 pink,24-26★)

Proverbs (31:10-12) --- Isaiah (1:16 blue) (33:15-16★)

Hosea (10:12★) --- Amos (5:14★★) --- Micah (6:8★★)

END OF OLD TESTAMENT

St. Matthew (5:16jw,48jw) --- St. Luke (3:14★) (6:19 pink)

I Corinthians (14:20 green,40 blue) --- II Corinthians (1:12★)

Galatians (6:9 blue) --- Ephesians (6:1-4 pink,8)

I Thessalonians (5:15 green,22★★) --- I Timothy (6:18)

Titus (3:2★★) --- Hebrews (13:16★★,21 green)

III John (1:11★★) --- Jude (1:8-15★)

Exodus (18:11 purple) --- Numbers (15:30 blue)

Deuteronomy (17:20★★) --- I Samuel (2:3 green)

Job (40:11-12 pink) --- Psalms (75:5★★)

Proverbs (6:16-19★★) (8:13★ angerlanguage) (11:2★) (16:19★★)

Proverbs (21:4★) (27:1 blue) (29:23★★)

Ecclesiastes (7:8★★)

Jeremiah (13:15★★) (49:15-16) (50:31 blue)

Ezekiel (28:1-9) --- Daniel (4:37 abase pride) (5:20 blue)

Obadiah (1:1-15★) --- Habakkuk (2:4★★)

END OF OLD TESTAMENT

St. Matthew (23:12 JW)

Romans (12:3 blue)

I Corinthians (4:6)

Galatians (6:3-4 green)

James (4:6★★)

THE SABBATH

Leviticus (25:8★★)

Deuteronomy (5:12★)

Isaiah (58:13-14★)

Jeremiah (17:21-22 green)

END OF OLD TESTAMENT

Genesis (28:3) --- Numbers (6:24-26 purple) (23:20 blue) (24:9)

Deuteronomy (11:26-28★) (15:6★★) (30:19 blue)

I Samuel (23:21★pink) --- II Samuel (7:29) --- I Kings (10:9★★)

I Chronicles (4:10★★) (16:36) (17:27★) (29:10-11★,20★)

II Chronicles (9:8 blue) --- Nehemiah (9:5-6 blue) (13:2 pink)

Job (22:24-28★) (37:14★★) (42:10 green) --- Psalms (1:1-3) (31:21)

Psalms (34:1 blue) (41:1-3) (66:20) (84:12) (113:2-3★✔)

Psalms (115:18 blue★) (118:26★★) (129:8★) (145:2 pink)

Proverbs (5:18-19 pink) --- Isaiah (1:19) (32:20 blue)

Jeremiah (17:7★) (49:31★) --- Malachi (3:10★)

END OF OLD TESTAMENT

St. Matthew (11:6JW) (23:39JW) --- St. Luke (7:23JW) (19:38)

St. Luke (24:50-53) --- St. John (20:29JW) --- Acts (20:35PW-JW)

Ephesians (1:3-4 pink) --- I Peter (3:9★) --- I John (3:22★★)

II John (1:8★) --- Revelation (1:3★★) (7:12 pink) (14:13)

I Samuel (12:23 pink) --- II Kings (6:17-23★) (20:1-11★life)

I Chronicles (4:10★★) (16:15) --- II Chronicles (6:40 blue)

II Chronicles (7:14 blue) (26:5★★) --- Ezra (6:10 green)

Job (33:26★★) (42:10 green) --- Psalms (5:3 blue,8 blue) (10:17★★)

Psalms (18:3 pink) (55:17 blue) (66:20) (90:14★) (96:7★✔)

Psalms (119:164 blue) (122:6-9 pink) --- Jeremiah (15:15★) (29:12-13★)

Ezekiel (46:13 blue)

END OF OLD TESTAMENT

St. Matthew (6:6-14jw, 33jw) (7:7-8jw) (17:15,16-18jw)

St. Matthew (21:13jw,21-22jw) --- St. Mark (6:12-13) (11:23-26jw)

St. Mark (14:38jw) --- St. Luke (11:9-10jw) (18:1,10-14jw) (19:46jw)

St. John (14:13-16jw) (16:22-24jw) (17:9-10jw,15-16jw)

Acts (6:4★★) --- Romans (1:9 blue) (10:1★,9,11★,12★★) (15:30-31 pink)

I Corinthians (14:15★) --- Ephesians (1:15-16 pink)

Colossians (4:2-3★) --- I Thessalonians (5:17,25)

I Timothy (2:8★) --- II Timothy (1:3 pink) --- James (5:13★★)

III John (1:2★★)

Exodus (23:13★,24-25 purple,32-33 purple) (34:14 green)

Leviticus (19:4) (26:1 green)

Deuteronomy (11:16★★)

Joshua (24:14★★,15,23★★)

II Kings (17:35-39,40-41 green)

Psalms (81:9-10★)

END OF OLD TESTAMENT

I John (5:21)

Genesis (6:3) (19:7 green) --- Exodus (22:21★)

Leviticus (8:32-35★✔ correct) --- Numbers (24:9)

Deuteronomy (4:9★,39-40★) (5:33★) (9:13-14★) (16:22) (18:10-12) (22:5★★)

Deuteronomy (24:16 green) (28:20 green) (30:15-16 blue✔) (33:23-24 green)

Judges (9:1-2) --- I Samuel (3:13★) (7:3★) (12:24★)

II Samuel (3:33-34 green★) --- I Kings (3:8-13★) (8:57 blue,60 blue)

I Chronicles (16:24 blue) --- II Chronicles (30:7★★)

Ezra (10:4★★,11) --- Esther (8:6) --- Job (4:8 green) (8:20★) (11:14-15★)

Job (16:19 blue) (27:3) (33:4) (36:21 green★ focus) --- Psalms (23:1★★)

Psalms (32:5-6 green) (35:9★✔) (49:7 green) (81:9-10★) (100:3★★)

Psalms (105:4 blue) (140:11 green) --- Proverbs (18:21 green) (23:7★)

Proverbs (24:13★,15,16 blue,17-19★★,29 green) (26:27 green) (28:9★,14★)

Proverbs (29:18) (30:32) --- Ecclesiastes (5:15)

Isaiah (1:16 blue) (3:10-12) (40:20★) (46:8★★) (49:9★) (51:18) (59:2★)

Jeremiah (2:32★★) (3:20) (4:14★★) (6:15-16★) (10:5,19 blue,24) (17:10★★,13★)

Jeremiah (31:30) (32:19★★) (45:5 green) (50:6 green,31 blue)

Lamentations (3:36,58-66) (5:1-3 green) --- Ezekiel (12:5-6★) (18:4-9★,20)

Ezekiel (22:14-16) (33:11★) (44:9) --- Daniel (4:27 accepted, 37 abase pride)

Daniel (5:10★★,20 blue) --- Hosea (4:11★★) --- Obadiah (1:15★)

Zechariah (1:4 green)   END OF OLD TESTAMENT

TURN TO NEXT PAGE TWENTY ➡

St. Matthew (6:14-15ᴊᴡ,24ᴊᴡ) (12:33ᴊᴡ,36-37ᴊᴡ)

St. Luke (17:1-4ᴊᴡ) (23:28ᴊᴡ,34ᴊᴡ) --- St. John (10:17-18ᴊᴡ ✓) (15:18ᴊᴡ)

Acts (8:36-37★★) (10:34-35★★) (13:10-11) (15:29★★) (16:31 green) (24:14-15★)

Romans (2:6-7★,25★,26-29) (5:19-21★★) (8:18★★,38-39★★) (11:22 blue)

Romans (12:1-3 blue) (13:1-2 green,8★,12-14★★) (14:7-10,13★) (15:3,7 pink)

I Corinthians (3:6-9★★,16-17 green) (4:5-6★,10★★) (6:20 pink) (13:11★)

I Corinthians (15:10★★,25-26★ no enemies,33-34,51-52)

II Corinthians (5:10 green,15★) (6:1-4★★) (9:6-7★★) (10:7 pink,12★★) (13:5-7★)

Galatians (2:16★,21) (6:3-4 green,✓7-8,14★,17 blue)

Ephesians (4:17-18★) --- Colossians (3:25) (4:6 pink)

I Thessalonians (5:15 green,17,25) --- I Timothy (5:1-2★,22★★)

II Timothy (1:6★★) --- Hebrews (9:28) (13:5,15)

James (1:22-25★★) (4:4,7-8★,15-17★★) (5:12,16 ★)

I Peter (4:1-2★,11★★,14-16) --- I John (5:4-13★★)

II Chronicles (30:9★★) --- Nehemiah (5:19 pink)

Psalms (23:6 pink) (77:7-9 pink,10-12 green) (85:1-7★★✔) (90:14★)

Psalms (103:8 pink) (116:5★) --- Proverbs (14:29-31 pink)

Hosea (6:6★★) --- Micah (6:8★★) (7:18-20 pink)

END OF OLD TESTAMENT

St. Matthew (7:12ᴊᴡ) (9:13ᴊᴡ) (17:15,16-18ᴊᴡ)

Acts (4:33 pink) --- Romans (1:7 blue) (6:14★★) (11:6★★ No Work)

Romans (16:24 pink) --- I Corinthians (1:3)

II Corinthians (12:9ʟᴡ) --- Galatians (1:3-5 pink)

Ephesians (2:7-9 pink) --- Colossians (4:6 pink) --- Hebrews (13:9)

James (4:6★★) --- II Peter (3:18★★) --- Jude (1:21 pink)

Exodus (15:2 purple) --- Deuteronomy (8:18★★)

II Samuel (6:14-22!) (22:1-51★ Davids psalm of thanksgiving)

I Chronicles (16:8,25,34-36) (23:20★★) --- Nehemiah (9:5-6 blue)

Psalms (5:11★) (7:17★★) (9:1★★) (18:3 pink) (21:13 pink) (28:7★★) (30:1,12)

Psalms (34:1 blue) (35:18) (44:8★★) (45:17 purple) (47:1★,7) (57:7-8 blue) (66:4)

Psalms (86:12★) (92:1★) (108:1-3★) (115:18 blue★) (119:62★,164 blue) (135:3)

Psalms (147:1★★) --- Proverbs (27:2) --- Isaiah (38:19 blue) (65:18)

Jeremiah (17:14★) (31:7 pink) --- Lamentations (3:41 pink)

Daniel (4:37 abase pride)

END OF OLD TESTAMENT

Romans (1:8 blue) (14:6) --- Ephesians (1:15-16 pink) (5:20 blue)

Colossians (3:17 green) --- I Thessalonians (5:18 pink)

II Timothy (1:3 pink) --- Hebrews (13:15) --- I Peter (3:3-4★)

Revelation (7:12 pink) (15:3 pink)

I Samuel (16:23 blue)

I Chronicles (16:9,23★) (47:1★,7)

I Chronicles (57:7-8 blue) (59:16-17★★)

Psalms (66:4) (81:1★) (92:1★)

Psalms (104:33-34) (108:1-3 ★) (135:3) (147:1 ★★) (149:5 ★★)

Isaiah (30:29★★)

Jeremiah (31:7 pink)

END OF OLD TESTAMENT

I Corinthians (14:15★)

Ephesians (5:19 pink)

Colossians (3:16 pink)

James (5:13★★)

Revelation (15:3 pink)

II Chronicles (13:12 green)

Job (4:8 green) (15:20 green)

Psalms (37:1-2 green)

Proverbs (21:4★) (24:15,16 blue)

Isaiah (29:15 green) (30:1-2★★) (66:4-5)

Jeremiah (21:13 green) (49:15-16)

Amos (9:2)

Zechariah (1:4 green)

END OF OLD TESTAMENT

St. Luke (22:64-65 blue 4 L Sake)

I Peter (2:1 green)

SANTIFICATION

Exodus (22:31★★) --- Leviticus (19:2★) (20:7-8) (21:4 pink) (22:32 pink)

Deuteronomy (5:12★) (7:6★) (14:2-3) --- Joshua (3:5★★)

I Chronicles (16:24 blue) --- II Chronicles (19:7 green) (29:5) (30:8)

Job (17:9★★) (22:21-23★) --- Psalms (4:3★✔) (29:2★★) (37:4-5★)

Psalms (145:17★★) --- Isaiah (8:13★★) (34:16-17)

Jeremiah (14:21 pink) --- Ezekiel (43:12★,26-27★)

Hosea (6:6★★) (10:12★) (12:6★★)

END OF OLD TESTAMENT

Romans (1:15-17 blue) (12:1-3 blue) (15:29-33 pink)

I Thessalonians (4:7 green,11-13★)

II Thessalonians (3:6★,9★,14-15★)

I Timothy (4:8 green) (6:6★★) --- II Timothy (2:15 blue,16★★)

Titus (2:12★★) --- I Peter (1:13-16) (4:1-2★,11★★,16)

Deuteronomy (20:1★★,4★★)

Joshua (1:5★★)

I Samuel (22:23 green)

II Chronicles (32:7-8★★)

Psalms (62:8★) (91:11) (105:14-15★★) (121:7,8 blue)

Isaiah (26:3-4★,20-21★) (43:1-2★★) (51:7,12) (54:17★★)

Jeremiah (1:19 blue) (39:18 green)

END OF OLD TESTAMENT

Exodus (21:12 green,14-15 green) --- Numbers (12:3 patient/mild) (30:2★)

Joshua (14:11) (24:15) --- I Samuel (15:23 green) (18:14) (21:15★ blue)

II Samuel (3:33-34 green★) --- I Kings (8:39★)

II Chronicles (1:10) (2:5★★,9★) --- Ezra (4:22 green) --- Job (27:6★★)

Job (28:28★★) (33:3,12-13 blue★,31-33★) (36:21 green★focus)

Psalms (29:3 blue) (32:8★✔) (37:27 green) (45:17 purple) (62:3) (68:34 blue)

Psalms (74:22 green) (90:12★) (104:15) (109:26-27★★) (112:7 green)

Psalms (118:17,24) --- Proverbs (1:8-9★★) (4:3-4 pink,7-9★★,23-26★)

Proverbs (6:20-23★★,25★★,32★) (8:13★ angerlanguage,19★ rest) (9:11-12 green)

Proverbs (10:1 pink,4 green,10) (11:1-2★,12 green,17★,27-31) (12:25 goodwords)

Proverbs (13:25) (14:7,13,29-31 pink,35★) (15:3 blue,27,33)

Proverbs (16:12-14★★,19-20★★) (17:25,28★) (18:7,21 green) (19:1,8,13)

Proverbs (20:29★) (21:9,19) (22:15★,24-26★) (23:7★,15-17★★) (24:29 green)

Proverbs (25:3★★) (27:1 blue,7 blue,11 blue) (28:9★,14★) (29:15★,17★,18)

Ecclesiastes (1:4,18) (4:9-11) (5:4-5★,12★,15) (7:1 pink,3★★,5,8★★,16-17)

Ecclesiastes (10:2) (12:12) --- Song of Solomon (8:3 pink,6 pink)

Isaiah (3:10-12) (5:11) (32:20 blue) (35:1-10) --- Jeremiah (5:5★)

Jeremiah (9:23-24★) (10:2★★) (14:7-10) (31:30) (32:33) (45:5 green)

Ezekiel (18:31-32) (33:11★) (45:10★★) --- Daniel (12:3 blue) --- Hosea (6:6★★)

Malachi (2:10 pink) (4:5-6)   END OF OLD TESTAMENT

TURN TO NEXT PAGE TWENTY SEVEN ➡

St. Matthew (6:27ᴊᴡ) (11:8) (19:5-9ᴊᴡ,21ᴊᴡ,29-30ᴊᴡ) (26:52ᴊᴡ)

St. Mark (4:24ᴊᴡ,30-32ᴊᴡ) --- St. Luke (9:58-62ᴊᴡ) (10:16ᴊᴡ) (11:17ᴊᴡ,39ᴊᴡ)

Romans (8:6,13) (9:32-33★★) (16:19 green)

I Corinthians (1:20,25,27-28 ★★,31) (3:10★) (4:19-21★) (5:6-8)

I Corinthians (7:1-5★,19,29,31,37) (10:10★,12★,14★,31-33 pink)

I Corinthians (11:3 green,7 green,9,13-17!,27-29 pink) (12:23-24,26 ★)

I Corinthians (14:38-39 green) (15:30-32 green)

II Corinthians (4:15-18★★) (5:18-21★) (8:9,11★) (10:12★★)

Galatians (3:13 green) (5:4★,6★,18★) --- Ephesians (4:13-15★) (5:15-17★)

Philippians (3:2) (4:11-12) --- Colossians (3:25) (4:5)

II Thessalonians (3:10-13) --- I Timothy (2:11-13★) (4:8 green)

I Timothy (5:21★) (6:7-8★,10 green,12 green) --- II Timothy (2:23★★)

James (4:14★★) --- I Peter (3:3-4★,17★★) --- II Peter (1:5-10★)

II Peter (2:11-12,21-22) (3:7-8★,18★★) --- I John (3:4 the Mosaic law)

II John (1:7-8★) --- Revelation (2:4-7ᴊᴡ) (7:12 pink) (13:18!) (15:4★)

Job (16:19 blue)

Psalms (10:17★★) (32:8★✔) (37:4-5★)

END OF OLD TESTAMENT

St. Matthew (17:20ᴊᴡ) (21:21-22ᴊᴡ)

Acts (14:22 blue)

Romans (1:8 blue,17 blue) (4:20-22) (10:17)

I Corinthians (2:5★★)

II Corinthians (5:7-8★)

Ephesians (3:17 pink)

I Timothy (6:12 green)

James (2:20 green,26 green)

RIGHTEOUS ANGER

Psalms (7:6-7 green) (74:22 green)

Habakkuk (3:12 green, 13-19 pink)

END OF OLD TESTAMENT

Genesis (50:17 pink)

Exodus (32:32 pink, 33-34 purple)

Numbers (14:19 pink)

I Kings (8:50 pink)

END OF OLD TESTAMENT

St. Matthew (6:14-15ᴊᴡ) (18:21-22ᴊᴡ, 35ᴊᴡ)

St. Mark (3:28-29ᴊᴡ) (11:25-26ᴊᴡ) --- St. Luke (5:20-26 forgiven)

St. Luke (17:1-4ᴊᴡ) (22:64-65 blue 4 L Sake) (23:34ᴊᴡ) (24:47ᴊᴡ)

St. John (20:23ᴊᴡ-forgive L.I.G.)

Acts (26:18★ᴊᴡ, 20★)

II Corinthians (2:9-11★★)

Ephesians (4:32★★)

Colossians (3:12-13 pink)

James (4:14★★)

Leviticus (25:17★★)

II Chronicles (32:7-8★★)

Esther (8:6)

Job (11:16-20★)

Psalms (37:1-2 green,7 green)

Proverbs (24:19★★)

END OF OLD TESTAMENT

St. Matthew (6:25 JW,31 JW)

St. John (14:1 JW,27-29 JW)

Deuteronomy (5:21★)

END OF OLD TESTAMENT

Acts (20:33★★)

Hebrews (13:5)

Ecclesiastes (7:3★★) (11:10 green)

Daniel (10:2-3)

END OF OLD TESTAMENT

II Corinthians (7:9-11)

PITY

I Samuel (23:21★pink)

Job (19:21 blue) (36:21 green★focus) (42:10 green)

Psalms (77:7-9 pink, 10-12 green)

Isaiah (55:7★)

Amos (6:6★★)

      END OF OLD TESTAMENT

I Peter (3:8 pink)

Genesis (50:21)

Exodus (22:28★)

I Samuel (8:8-9)

I Kings (12:7 omw)

II Chronicles (10:7 pink omw)

Nehemiah (5:19 pink)

Job (2:10★)

Psalms (34:13-14★★) (63:3 pink) (140:11 green)

Proverbs (8:8★) (12:25 goodwords)

Ezekiel (45:9 green)

    END OF OLD TESTAMENT

Ephesians (4:32★★)

Colossians (3:8,20 pink,21)

Titus (3:2★★)

Hebrews (13:16★★,21 green)

Leviticus (19:35-36 blue) --- Deuteronomy (11:18-21★★) (22:6-7) (24:5)

Deuteronomy (30:15-16 blue✔) --- I Chronicles (16:11-12)

Job (13:19 blue) (27:6★★) (33:4,12-13 blue★) (36:21 green★ focus)

Psalms (23:6 pink) (31:1) (35:9★✔) (37:27 green) (63:3 pink) (90:12 ★,14 ★)

Psalms (142:7★★) --- Proverbs (8:35 green) --- Ecclesiastes (9:4★)

Song of Solomon (1:13 pink) (8:14 pink) --- Isaiah (1:16 blue)

Jeremiah (39:18 green) (45:5 green) --- Lamentations (5:1-3 green)

Micah (6:1 green,8★★)

END OF OLD TESTAMENT

St. John (8:31-32jw) (16:1jw,20jw,33jw) --- I Corinthians (9:24-27)

I Corinthians (14:20 green,40 blue) (15:30-32 green)

II Corinthians (9:6-7★★) --- Galatians (2:17-20)

Philippians (1:20-21★★,28-29★★) (4:21 pink) --- Colossians (1:10 pink)

I Thessalonians (5:16★★) --- II Timothy (1:6★★) (4:5★★,6-8)

Hebrews (12:1★,12-14★) --- Jude (1:21 pink)

II Kings (19:34 green)

II Chronicles (32:7-8★★)

Psalms (119:45-46 green,80★★) (142:7★★)

Proverbs (6:5★)

Isaiah (49:9★) (61:1-2 green,10)

Jeremiah (39:18 green) (45:5 green) (52:31-34)

Micah (6:1 green)

END OF OLD TESTAMENT

St. John (8:31-32 JW)

II Corinthians (3:17 green)

Galatians (5:1 green,13-14 pink)

Hebrews (13:1-2 pink,8 blue)

I Peter (2:15-16 green)

Revelation (21:6)

ENEMIES

38

II Kings (17:35-39)

Psalms (110:1★)

Proverbs (20:22 green) (25:21★★)

END OF OLD TESTAMENT

St. Matthew (5:44jw) (22:44jw)

Genesis (1:3-4) --- Exodus (34:29-30★ no vagueness)

I Samuel (14:27★★) --- II Samuel (23:3-4★) --- Nehemiah (5:19 pink)

Job (25:5) (31:28-30) (33:12-13 blue★) --- Psalms (19:1 blue,8-11★) (35:9★✔)

Psalms (37:27 green) (80:1-7★,19★★) (105:4 blue) (144:14-15★★ no complaining)

Proverbs (8:35 green) (15:30★) (21:29) (22:9 pink) (25:21★★)

Ecclesiastes (11:7★✔) --- Isaiah (2:5★✔) (60:19-20) --- Daniel (12:3 blue)

END OF OLD TESTAMENT

St. Matthew (5:16ᴊw) (6:22ᴊw) (7:5ᴊw) --- St. Luke (11:34-36ᴊw✔)

St. John (8:12ᴊw,42ᴊw) (9:4-5ᴊw) (11:9-10ᴊw) (12:35-36ᴊw) (15:4-8ᴊw★)

Acts (26:18ᴊw★) --- Romans (9:25-26,28) (12:8★★ be nice) (13:12-14★★)

I Corinthians (15:30-32 green) --- Ephesians (1:18 pink) (4:1-2 green,24★★)

Ephesians (5:8★★,11 green,14★★)

Colossians (3:1,2 pink,12-16 pink,17 green,23-24 pink)

I Thessalonians (5:6 green,8 green,11,16★★) --- II Timothy (1:6★★)

Titus (3:2★★) --- Hebrews (9:28) (10:22★★) (13:1-2 pink, 3★, 9, 21 green)

James (1:22-25★★) --- I Peter (1:23★★) (3:3-4★)

I John (1:5★) (3:22★★) --- Jude (1:8-15★,21 pink)

Revelation (3:19ᴊw) (21:6) (22:14-15 green,17)

Genesis (45:5★★) --- Exodus (14:14 purple) (23:30 blue) --- Ruth (2:12 green)

I Samuel (12:23 pink) (26:24★) --- II Samuel (3:39 green)

I Kings (8:57 blue,60 blue) --- II Kings (19:19 blue)

I Chronicles (21:12-14) --- II Chronicles (15:12-15★★) (20:17) (26:5★★)

II Chronicles (30:7★★) (31:21★) (32:7-8★★) --- Job (1:22) (8:6-9★)

Job (11:16-20★) (13:15 blue) (16:19 blue) (33:12-13 blue★) (37:14★★)

Psalms (5:8 blue,11★) (10:17★★) (16:8-11) (23:1★★,4) (25:2 green) (26:11)

Psalms (27:1★,9★,14★★) (28:7★★) (31:1,3★★,5-6★,15 green,16★★) (32:8★✔)

Psalms (35:9★✔) (37:4-5★) (46:10 blue) (55:22-23★) (62:8★,10)

Psalms (71:1★★,14★★,18★★) (84:12) (109:26-27★★) (110:1★) (112:7 green)

Psalms (118:6,8-9) (119:165 pink) (121:1 green) (143:10★★) (147:10-11)

Proverbs (16:3★★,19-20★★) (20:22 green) (21:31) (31:10-12)

Isaiah (26:3-4★,20-21★) (31:1★★,6 green) (42:13-14) (50:6-8 green)

Isaiah (51:9-11 blue) (59:17-18 green) --- Jeremiah (1:19 blue) (17:5★)

Jeremiah (32:17★★,27★★) (39:18 green) --- Hosea (12:6★★)

Joel (2:12-15 green) --- Micah (7:6-7) --- Habakkuk (2:1-4★★)

END OF OLD TESTAMENT

St. Matthew (6:25JW,31JW,33JW) (11:28-30JW) (19:26JW) (22:44JW)

St. Luke (1:37★) (10:17 green) --- Acts (5:29★) (14:22 blue)

Romans (16:20 green) --- II Corinthians (12:10 pink,11-12)

TURN TO NEXT PAGE FORTY ➡

Ephesians (6:10-17 green)

Philippians (1:20-21★★,28-29★★) (3:20-21 blue)

Philippians (4:13 green,19)

I Timothy (6:17 green)

II Timothy (3:14-17)

Hebrews (6:12 green)

James (4:14★★)

Revelation (22:11)

Joshua (1:6-7★★,9★)

I Kings (2:1-3★)

I Chronicles (19:13★) (28:20) (29:1★★)

II Chronicles (15:7★) (31:21★)

Psalms (24:7-9 pink) (31:24★) (80:1-7★,19★) (144:14-15★★ no complaining)

Daniel (10:19 blue)

Joel (3:10 green)

END OF OLD TESTAMENT

Romans (4:19)

I Corinthians (16:13★★)

Galatians (6:9 blue)

Ephesians (6:10-17 green)

II Timothy (2:1★★,3★★)

Leviticus (19:15-16) --- Deuteronomy (1:17 green) --- I Samuel (16:7)

II Chronicles (1:10) --- Nehemiah (5:19 pink) --- Job (16:19 blue)

Psalms (7:8-9★★) (10:18★★) (62:3) (75:6-7★★)

Ecclesiastes (11:9 green) (12:14★★) --- Isaiah (33:22★★)

Habakkuk (1:12-13 blue)

   END OF OLD TESTAMENT

St. Matthew (7:1-2ᴊᴡ) --- St. John (7:24ᴊᴡ) (8:14-16ᴊᴡ,50-51ᴊᴡ)

Romans (2:1 green) (14:13★) --- I Corinthians (5:13 green) (11:31-32 green)

II Corinthians (10:7 pink,12★★) --- I Timothy (5:21★)

James (4:11-12★) (5:9★)

Deuteronomy (25:13-15) --- II Kings (22:19-20 pink)

II Chronicles (7:14 blue) (12:6★pink★) --- Job (37:14★★)

Psalms (4:4★★) (10:17★★) (35:13 green) --- Proverbs (11:1-2★)

Proverbs (14:29-31 pink) (15:33) (16:19★★) (22:4★★) (27:2) (29:23★★)

Ecclesiastes (7:8★★) --- Isaiah (5:15) (57:15-16 ★)

Jeremiah (13:18★) --- Lamentations (3:25 pink) --- Micah (6:8★★)

END OF OLD TESTAMENT

St. Matthew (23:12 ᴊᴡ) --- St. John (6:14-15 green★ Humility★)

Acts (8:32-35) --- James (4:6★★,9-10★)

I Peter (5:5★,6-8 pink,10 pink)

Genesis (28:22★★)

Exodus (35:5 purple,8 pink)

Leviticus (9:7 pink✔) (22:21 blue)

I Chronicles (29:3,17★)

II Chronicles (2:4) (13:11)

Ezra (6:10 green)

Psalms (20:3★★) (76:11 green) (116:18)

Isaiah (43:23-24★)

Ezekiel (46:13 blue)

Malachi (3:8,10★)

 END OF OLD TESTAMENT

Hebrews (7:2★)

VAINGLORY

Proverbs (30:32)

Isaiah (65:23★★)

END OF OLD TESTAMENT

Philippians (2:3 blue)

Genesis (28:21 pink) --- Judges (6:23 pink) (18:5-6★★)

I Samuel (10:27 pink) (25:6 pink) --- Nehemiah (5:19 pink)

Psalms (4:4★★) (37:11 green) (85:8★★) (120:7 blue) (122:6-9 pink)

Proverbs (11:12 green) (16:7 pink) --- Isaiah (26:3-4★,20-21★) (48:22)

Isaiah (57:2,19★,21) --- Jeremiah (29:7★★)

Zechariah (8:16-17 green)

END OF OLD TESTAMENT

St. Mark (9:50 JW) --- St. Luke (2:14 pink) (10:5 JW) (19:38,40,42 JW)

Acts (10:36 pink) --- Romans (1:7 blue) (14:19 blue) (15:33 pink)

I Corinthians (1:3) (14:33 pink) --- Galatians (1:3-5 pink)

Ephesians (4:3 pink) --- Colossians (3:15 pink)

I Peter (5:14 pink) --- III John (1:14★★)

Leviticus (16:29,31,34 ★)

II Kings (20:1-11★ life)

Job (36:21 green★ focus)

Psalms (30:2) (126:5 blue)

Daniel (10:2-3)

     END OF OLD TESTAMENT

St. Luke (23:28 JW)

St. John (11:35)

James (4:9-10★)

Deuteronomy (15:7-11★)

Job (42:10 green)

Psalms (121:1 green)

Ecclesiastes (4:9-11)

Isaiah (58:10★★)

Genesis (49:14-15★)

Psalms (4:4★★) (27:14★★) (31:24★)

Psalms (37:4-5★,7 green) (46:10 blue)

Proverbs (20:22 green)

Isaiah (18:4 blue) (30:15★★,18★★) (40:31 blue) (57:19★)

Jeremiah (47:6★)

Lamentations (3:25 pink)

Hosea (6:1-2★★)

END OF OLD TESTAMENT

St. Matthew (11:28-30ᴊᴡ)

Hebrews (12:1★)

James (5:7-8★)

Judges (8:2★★)

I Samuel (21:15★ blue)

Job (40:11 pink)

Psalms (37:8 green)

Isaiah (37:28-29 blue)

Ezekiel (45:9 green)

END OF OLD TESTAMENT

Ephesians (4:26★)

Colossians (3:8)

Genesis (33:8)

Numbers (14:11-12)

Judges (8:5★★)

I Samuel (12:23 pink)

II Kings (6:17-23★)

II Chronicles (1:10-12)

END OF OLD TESTAMENT

St. Matthew (8:1-4ᴊᴡ) (15:8-9ᴊᴡ)

Galatians (2:6-8,14-15) (3:13 green)

Genesis (45:5★★) --- I Samuel (8:7-9) --- Psalms (142:7★★)

Psalms (144:14-15★★ no complaining) (145:2 pink)

Proverbs (6:5★) (14:7) (20:13★) (22:29 pink) --- Isaiah (43:18-19★★)

Isaiah (62:10 blue) (65:16-17★) --- Jeremiah (1:7-8★★,17★) (49:31★)

Ezekiel (12:5-6★) --- Daniel (5:10★★) --- Micah (6:1 green)

END OF OLD TESTAMENT

St. Matthew (4:10ᴊᴡ★) (16:23ᴊᴡ) --- St. Luke (9:61-62ᴊᴡ)

Romans (10:1★,9,11★,12★★) (16:17) --- I Corinthians (13:11★)

II Corinthians (5:17 blue) (8:10 blue,12★) --- Galatians (6:17 blue)

Philippians (3:13-14★★) --- I Thessalonians (2:12★★)

II Timothy (1:6★★) (2:16★★,23★★) (4:9 blue)

Hebrews (12:1★,12-14★) --- Revelation (22:11)

Isaiah (58:4-8★)

Joel (2:12-15 green)

END OF OLD TESTAMENT

St. Matthew (6:16-18ᴊᴡ)

Genesis (13:8)

Exodus (21:23-25★★)

Proverbs (17:1★) (19:13) (21:9,19)

Lamentations (3:36)

END OF OLD TESTAMENT

St. Matthew (5:39ᴊᴡ)

Philippians (2:14)

Exodus (2:25 ★ pink)

Leviticus (19:30,32) (26:2 blue)

Deuteronomy (5:16★)

I Samuel (2:30★★)

I Chronicles (29:12-16★,18-19★)

Nehemiah (5:19 pink)

Psalms (18:3 pink) (19:14★) (35:28★) (37:23★) (66:4) (71:14★★)

Psalms (92:10 pink) (119:15-16★★)

END OF OLD TESTAMENT

St. Matthew (7:12 JW) (13:57 JW)

St. Mark (6:4 JW)

St. John (8:49 JW)

Ephesians (6:2-3 pink)

Colossians (1:10 pink)

I Peter (2:17 green)

Revelation (7:12 pink)

I Samuel (2:8-10★★) --- I Chronicles (16:10,27-29 ★) --- Job (40:10 pink)

Psalms (19:1 blue) (21:13 pink) (29:2★★) (35:28★) (37:23★) (46:10 blue)

Psalms (92:10 pink) (96:7★✔) (113:2-3★✔) (149:5★★)

Isaiah (12:6★★) (24:15★★) (55:5 green) (60:15)

Lamentations (3:41 pink)

END OF OLD TESTAMENT

St. Luke (2:14 pink) --- St. John (12:28ᴊᴡ)

Romans (4:20-22) (5:3-5★★) (16:27 green)

I Corinthians (1:31) (3:21★★)

II Corinthians (1:20 blue★) (10:17★★) (12:9ᴊᴡ)

Ephesians (3:21 blue) --- I Peter (3:3-4★) (4:11★★,14-16) (5:11 pink)

II Peter (3:18★★) --- Revelation (7:12 pink)

II Samuel (19:7★) (24:14★★)

Isaiah (40:1★★) (54:11) (66:10-14 The New Jerusalem)

ENDOFOLDTESTAMENT

II Corinthians (1:6-7 pink) (7:4★)

II Thessalonians (2:17 blue)

The Section Here Are Generations Building Up To Us And

The Age Of Gods Earth Existence By Adding The Numbers

Adam at 130 yrs. old begat Seth, Seth at 105 yrs. old begat Enos,

Enos at 90 yrs. old begat Cainan, Cainan at 70 yrs. old begat Mahalaleel,

Mahalaleel at 65 yrs. old begat Jared, Jared at 162 yrs. old begat Enoch,

Enoch at 65 yrs. old begat Methuselah, Methuselah at 187 yrs. old begat Lamech,

Lamech at 182 yrs. old begat Noah, Noah at 500 yrs. old begat Shem, Ham, & Japheth,

Shem at 100 yrs. old begat Arphaxad two years after God sent the flood.

Arphaxad at 35 yrs. old begat Salah, Salah at 30 yrs. old begat Eber,

Eber at 34 yrs. old begat Peleg, Peleg at 30 yrs. old begat Reu,

Reu at 32 yrs. old begat Serug, Serug at 30 yrs. old begat Nahor,

Nahor at 29 yrs. old begat Terah, Terah at 70 yrs. old begat Abram (Abraham),

Abraham at 100 yrs. old begat Isaac, Isaac at 60 yrs. old begat Esau & Jacob (twins),

Around Year 2044 B.C. At This Time

Jacob (Israel) between 90 & 100 yrs. old begat Joseph,

Joseph between age 47 & 80 yrs. old begat Jesus. Joseph died at 110 yrs. old.

I'll say the Earth is between 4200 & 4300 yrs. old

Earth is between 4200 & 4300 yrs. old

The Next Page Truths From The Bible Has Clues To Help For This Page ➡

The List Here Are Truths From The Bible For The

Prior Page To Help You Find The People And Truths

Genesis Chapter 5 Adam – Noah at 500 yrs. old begat Shem, Ham, & Japeth

Genesis Chapter 11 Shem – Terah at 70 yrs. old begat Abram (Abraham)

Genesis Chapter 17 Abram Name Changed To Abraham

Genesis Chapter 21:5 Abraham was 100 yrs. old, when his son Isaac was born unto him.

Genesis Chapter 25 Isaac at 60 yrs. old begat Esau & Jacob (twins)

           Abraham died at 175 yrs. old.

Genesis Chapter 30 Jacob begat Joseph from Rachel, I read.

Genesis Chapter 35:28 Isaac died at 180 yrs. old, Joseph around 15 yrs. old at

        this time, Jacob (Israel) was 114 yrs. old at this time.

Genesis Chapter 37:2 Joseph seventeen yrs. old

Genesis Chapter 41:50-51 Joseph at age 30 had firstborn Manasseh, Manasseh

        is Jesus Brother, look in book Ezekiel Chapter 48.

Genesis Chapter 47 Jacob 130 & 147 yrs. old

Genesis Chapter 49:33 Jacob (Israel) dies at 147 yrs. old,

        Joseph around 47 yrs. old at this time.

Genesis Chapter 50:26 Joseph died at 110 yrs. old

St. Matthew Chapter 1 The Birth of Jesus Christ

St. Luke Chapter 2:42 Jesus was 12 yrs. old, parents went looking for him.

St. Luke Chapter 3:23 Jesus began to be about 30 yrs. old

This Section Here Are Truths To Elevate Your Knowledge

In book Ezekiel Manasseh was mentioned in Chapter 48 which is

Josephs firstborn, Jesus brother.

Josephs firstborn Manasseh, Manasseh firstborn Machir which is the

Father of Gilead. /Adam at 130 yrs. old begat Seth.

Adam lived 800 yrs. after he begat Seth.

Jesus went to a city called Nain / Jericho the city of palm trees.

Jacob (Israel) had many children before Joseph, 11 from different women.

Gideon altar in Ophrah of the Abiezrites / The Heap of A.I.

Unto this day Bashanhavothjair / Sihor before Egypt

Havothjair unto this day in the land of Gilead.

Judges chapter 10 this should be around after 200 A.D.

Judges chapter 13 around 300 A.D., Over 360 A.D. after the book Ruth.

Joshua the son of Nun / Gods dwelling place Zion.

Noah was 500 yrs. old and had Shem, Ham, & Japheth.

Shem was 100 yrs. old and had Arphaxad 2 yrs. after the flood.

Shem lived 500 yrs. after he had Arphaxad.

Flood destroyed the Earth around or in 1654 B.C.

MORE TRUTHS ON THE NEXT PAGE ⟹

More Truths To Elevate Your Knowledge

I Kings chapter 6   418th year after the children came out of the land of Egypt.

Moses & God brought them out around 100 A.D.

Moses was born of one of Levi's daugthers, Levi is Jacobs 3rd son.◄Exodus chapter 2.

32 thousand Israelites Judges chapter 7 Jacobs kin in A.D.

Jacob is Davids 9th greatgrandfather / David dwelt in a city Ariel

Jesse is Davids dad (the youngest) / David is Solomons dad

Noahs Ark rested on the mountains of Ararat. / Mount Si-nai god spoke

David died at 70 around 515 A.D. / Jesus mentions King David in St. Luke chapter 20.

I Kings chapter 15 around 600 A.D. reign after Asa 40 years.

I Kings after Ahab chapter 16 around 620 A.D.

II Kings chapter 12 Jehoash begin to reign for Judah around 700 A.D.

St. Luke chapter 3 (generations made by God)

Abraham rejoiced to see Jesus day (birth) St. John chapter 8:56

Peter denied Jesus 3 times then the cock crew / Judas Iscariot betrayed Jesus.

Look up a penny with Caesar on it? spoken about in book St. Luke chapter 20.

River Parted Unto <u>Four</u> in Eden

1 Pison – Havilah

2 Gihon – Ethiopia

3 Hiddekel – Assyria

4 Euphrates

End Of Some Truths From The Bible

This Section Is A List Of All And Only Months

In My Bible That I've Read And Discovered

Nisan (1st month)

Zif (2nd month)

Sivan (3rd month)

Ethanim (7th month)

Bul (8th month)

Chisleu (9th month)

Tebeth (10th month)

Sebat (11th month)

Adar (12th month)

Abib (   ) not mentioned

Elul (   ) not mentioned

This Section Here Are Different Cities In The Bible I'll Love

To Check Off By Finding Them From A Globe Or Computer

Kadesh	Thyatira	Jehovahjireh	Nineveh
Ashdod	Amphipolis	Gerar	Rehoboth
Oboth	Apollonia	Avith	Calah
Judea	Thessalonica	Gibeon	Resen
Ijeabarim	Chios	Ramah	Babel
Moab	Samos	Luz	Bethel
Mattanah	Trogyllium	Makkedah	Sodom
Nahaliel	Miletus	Edrei	Canaan
Bamoth	Coos	Salchah	Hebron
Israel	Rhodes	Bashan	Shur
Judah	Patara	Argob	Elath
Perezuzza	Antipatris	Meribah	Beersheba
Mysia	Myra	Massah	Rameses
Troas	Lasea	Horeb	Succoth
Bitynia	Island Clauda	Rephidim	Sinai
Macedonia	Rhegium	Ephesus	Paran
Rome	Puteoli	Shinar	Chephirah
Samothracia	Dalmatia	Asshur	Beeroth
Neapolis			

TURN TO NEXT PAGE FOR MORE CITIES ➡

More Cities In The Bible

Kirjathjearim	Eziongeber	Nain	Cyrene
Gilgal	Eloth	Bethsaida	Charran
Belial	Edom	Emmaus	Cyprus
Island Crete	Damascus	Bethabara	Madian
Ziklag	Samaria	Cana	Wilderness of
Ramoth	Assyria	Enon	Mount Sina
Jattir	Syria	Salim	Tarsus
Aroer	Uz	Salem	Lydda
Siphmoth	Magdala	Sychar	Saron
Eshtemoa	Galilee	Jerusalem	Joppa
Rachal	Bethany	Mesopotamia	Phenice
Hormah	Gethsemane	Cappadocia	Antioch
Chorashan	Arimathaēa	Pontus	Seleucia
Athach	Decapolis	Asia	Salamis
Geba	Gennesaret	Phrygia	Iconium
Helam	Dalmanutha	Pamphylia	Lystra
Jericho	Ituraēa	Egypt	Derbe
Rabbah	Trachonitis	Libya	Lycaonia
Bahurim	Abilene		

END OF MOST THE CITIES TO FIND FROM THE BIBLE

This Section I Point Out Gods Feasts
And Holy Convocations That's Located
In The Book Leviticus Chapter 23

<u>Gods Feasts</u>   January 14th is The Lords Passover

February 14th is The Lords 2nd Passover. You should eat unleavened

bread that day and bitter herbs.

January 15th Sabbath & January 21st Sabbath, Holy Convocations: an offering

made by fire unto the Lord January 15th – January 21st, 7 days you must eat unleavened bread.

July 1st Sabbath; A memorial of blowing of trumpets. A Holy Convocation.

July 9th even, from even unto even, shall you celebrate your sabbath.

July 10th Day of Atonement: it shall be an holy convocation unto you: and you shall

afflict your souls, it shall be unto you a sabbath of rest, and you shall afflict your souls.

July 15th Sabbath; Holy Convocation unto you a solemn assembly, offer made by fire unto the Lord.

July 15th – July 21st; The Feasts of Tabernacles for 7 Days unto the Lord.

Offering made by fire unto God; REJOICE REJOICE REJOICE; for 7 days.

You shall dwell in booths and celebrate The Lord

Your God who brought you out of the land of Egypt.

July 22nd Sabbath; Holy Convocation unto you a solemn assembly, offer made by fire unto the Lord.

And These Shall Be Statutes For Ever Throughout Our Generations. GW

Extras
Saturday February 17, 2018 10:15 pm thru Sunday February 18, 2018 12:30 am

It took me from mid-June to mid-September 2014 to write and peace

Choices Out The Good Book pages together.

For every individual soul I Damitri has got some more valuable information

for us. At 27 and a half years old I was told to read Psalms and Proverbs, so I

started reading them, after-mid September thru mid-October 2011, then I read

Revelation the next few weeks; jotting bit scripture and chapters, after that,

I started reading the whole bible from the beginning doing the same. When I

got to Psalms and Proverbs I didn't read them again, but I read Revelation

again; when I finally got to it. Around this time it was after-mid of

January 2012. The second time I started reading the bible was mid-February

thru before-mid May 2012. The third time I started was after-mid May thru

after-mid August 2012. That's three times in eleven months jotting bit scripture

and chapters learning words and it's definitions, meaning of that word; reading

the definition of it with the scripture, chapters, different stories that's

in the bible; I was learning it, words after words after more words.

Three more times I read it and I was still writing and learning.

Around this time it was after-mid December 2013. Then one more time

March 20, 2014 thru May 19, 2014. Just 61 days; Doing the same; Accumulating info;

Researching trying to piece things. Seven times in a span of 32 months.

MORE EXTRAS

➡

More Extras

Also, you need to know that it says you need to study to show

yourself worthy. And this is true because sometimes we go days

without prayer to God. Some weeks, some months, maybe even years.

"Lets All Have Love For All". "Peace, Charity, And Freedom For All".

"Respect For All". "And Practice Mosaic And The Law".

CHOICES

OUT

THE

GOOD

BOOK

FROM A LEARNERS JOURNAL *DLF*

Sketches

The 5 Sketches I'd drawn are from the clouds; And this is in a 2 week-span;

From mid-July 2012 to about the end of July 2012 I watched the sky searching

for Gods face in the sky, and him holding Jesus in his right hand (a truth from the

bible). Also Gods holy angels are always ascending and descending through the clouds.

Now you'll see in the 1st sketch was during the daytime; I was standing out

front of my house on the driveway, and in the sky I seen God holding Jesus;

and to the right it was the sun. This image lasted only 30 to 45 seconds because

the rapid clouds. (Rapid meaning moving or occurring with speed; swift;) After

that I stepped inside got a piece of paper sat at the table and drew the image.

Now the next, the 2nd sketch was also during the daytime; I was standing out

front of my house on the driveway, and in the sky I'll say it was Jesus I'd seen

holding I guess a ropelike string stretching to the sun, and in his other arm

I'll say it looked like he's pulling a bag or chest maybe filled with food or gifts.

This image lasted 45 seconds, but from 5 to 45 seconds this image stretched

as the clouds moved. (This image got taller). After that I stepped inside got the

same piece of paper sat at the table and drew it underneath the first image.

MORE OF SKETCHES
⟹

95

More Sketches

Now you'll see in the 3rd sketch was during the nighttime; I was standing out

back of my house on the porch, and in the sky I seen God holding Jesus.

This image lasted 2 minutes. After that I stepped inside got the same

piece of paper I flipped it over sat at the table and drew it.

Now you'll see in the 4th sketch was during the daytime; I was driving home

in my car and in the sky way out in front of me I seen God holding Jesus.

This image lasted 3 minutes. I got home 10 minutes after, stepped in got the same

piece of paper I'd flipped over; sat at the table and drew it under the third image.

Now you'll see in the 5th sketch was during the daytime; I was standing out

back of my house on the porch, and in the sky I seen a big image of the face of God;

and he looked wroth. (Wroth meaning angry). This image lasted 1 minute 10 seconds

to 1 minute 25 seconds. After that I stepped inside and got a new

piece of paper sat at the table and drew the image.

Sketches Sunday am. March 4, 2018

by

Damitri Franklin

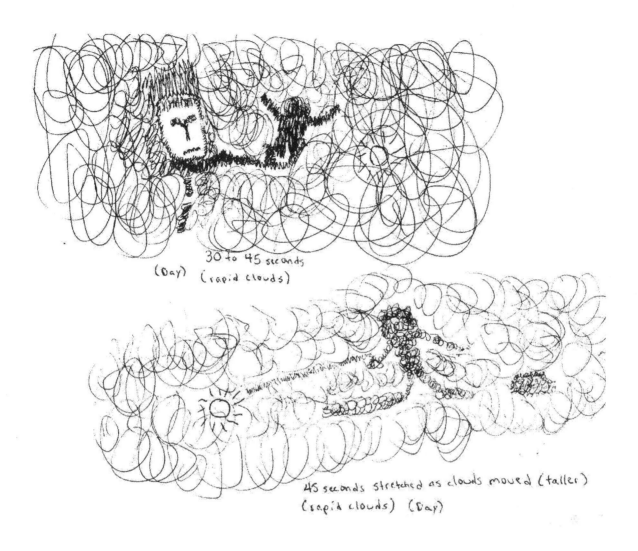

30 to 45 seconds
(Day)   (rapid clouds)

45 seconds stretched as clouds moved (taller)
(rapid clouds) (Day)

2.00 minute
(Night)

(Day) 3 minutes

Big Image
minute: 10 to 1:25 secon.
(Worst Image) (Day)

CONCLUSION

By

Damitri Lashawn Franklin

Now this concludes the Choices Out The Good Book that I've provided for you

by the helping hand of Our Heavenly Father God. I hope this motivates and inspires

every single human being in the world to be followers of Our Lord And Savior

Jesus Christ. Let God, Peace, Love, Joy, Forgiveness, and Righteousness Be With

Us All. To every single individual soul, Have the Love of God in your Heart, and

let these choices improve your spiritual development to make the whole world

a better place. Let's keep discrimination far from our thoughts and any type

of slavery far from our thoughts and better your ownselves. But also better

the people around you, don't bring them down with harsh words or harsh

entrapments, and to every individual --- Think, Speak, Do, and Act Good.

God knows everything we do, and through time every individual will be

repaid for their goodness or their iniquity, so please, choose goodness.

Jesus Christ Our Lord And Savior To All, Let His Spirit

Guide Us And Walk With Us All On Gods Earth.

May The Blessings Of God Be On Us All, Peace And Goodwill Toward All Mankind

Analyzed and Peaced by *Damitri Franklin* Bless You

100

Printed in the United States
By Bookmasters